S.S.F Public Library
West Orange
840 West Orange Ave.
South San Francisco, CA 94080

South San Francisco Public Library

Y0-BZJ-504

2

SEP 21

Sign Language & Family

Bela Davis

Abdo Kids Junior
is an Imprint of Abdo Kids
abdobooks.com

Abdo
EVERYDAY SIGN LANGUAGE
Kids

abdobooks.com

Published by Abdo Kids, a division of ABDO, P.O. Box 398166, Minneapolis, Minnesota 55439.
Copyright © 2022 by Abdo Consulting Group, Inc. International copyrights reserved in all countries.
No part of this book may be reproduced in any form without written permission from the publisher.
Abdo Kids Junior™ is a trademark and logo of Abdo Kids.

Printed in the United States of America, North Mankato, Minnesota.

052021

092021

THIS BOOK CONTAINS
RECYCLED MATERIALS

Photo Credits: Shutterstock

Production Contributors: Teddy Borth, Jennie Forsberg, Grace Hansen

Design Contributors: Candice Keimig, Pakou Moua

Library of Congress Control Number: 2020947656

Publisher's Cataloging-in-Publication Data

Names: Davis, Bela, author.

Title: Sign language & family / by Bela Davis

Description: Minneapolis, Minnesota : Abdo Kids, 2022 | Series: Everyday sign language | Includes online
    resources and index.

Identifiers: ISBN 9781098207014 (lib. bdg.) | ISBN 9781098207854 (ebook) | ISBN 9781098208271
    (Read-to-Me ebook)

Subjects: LCSH: American Sign Language--Juvenile literature. | Family--Juvenile literature. | Family life--
    Juvenile literature. | Deaf--Means of communication--Juvenile literature. | Language acquisition--
    Juvenile literature.

Classification: DDC 419--dc23

Table of Contents

Signs and Family

ASL is a visual language. There is a sign for the whole family!

FAMILY

1. Make the "F" sign with both hands holding them up near torso

2. Form a circle with both hands ending with pinkies touching away from the body

Tess and her dad brush their teeth.

DAD

1. Open hand with all five fingers spread out

2. Tap forehead with thumb, pinky pointing away from face

7

Sam's mom got him a new shirt. It has pineapples on it!

MOM

1. Open hand with all five fingers spread out
2. Tap chin with thumb, pinky pointing away from face

9

James reads with his grandma.

It's his favorite book.

GRANDMA

1. Open hand with all five fingers spread out
2. Touch chin with thumb, pinky pointing away from face
3. Bounce hand away from face

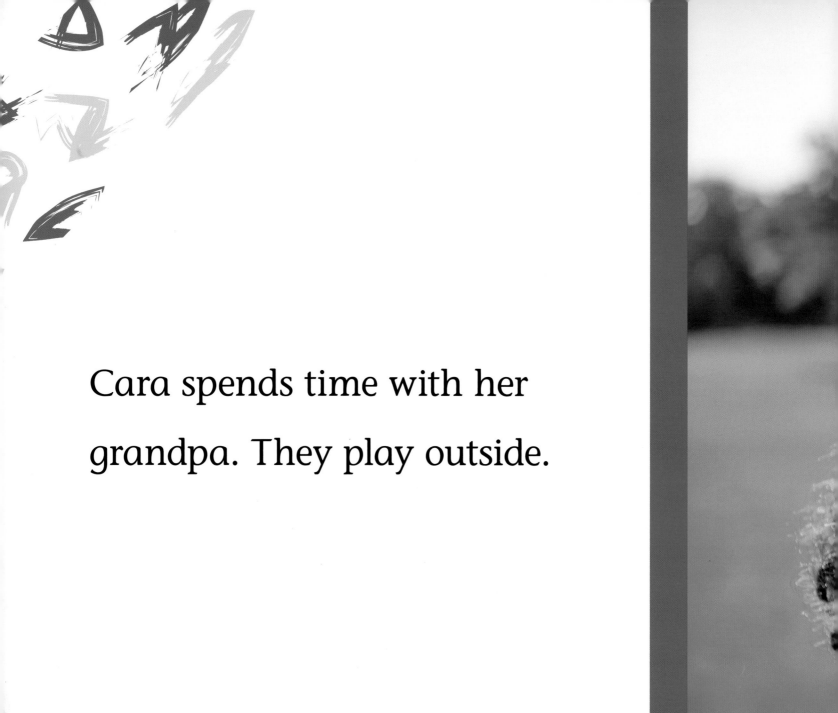

Cara spends time with her grandpa. They play outside.

GRANDPA

1. Open hand with all five fingers spread out
2. Tap forehead with thumb, pinky pointing away from face
3. Bounce hand away from face

13

Hana and her aunt
have a special day.
They explore the city.

AUNT

1. Make the "A" sign
2. Bring hand up so your thumb is near your cheek
3. Make a small circle motion

Rico's uncle is funny!

UNCLE

1. Make the "U" sign
2. Bring hand up to forehead
3. Make a small circle motion

17

Lea and Mae love

their brother.

BROTHER

1. Make two "L" hands
2. Tap one "L" hand to forehead, while other sits below
3. Bring hand down to meet other hand, stacking them

19

Bella has ice cream with her sister Ella.

SISTER

1. Make two "L" hands
2. Tap one "L" hand to chin, while other sits below
3. Bring hand down to meet other hand, stacking them

21

The ASL Alphabet!

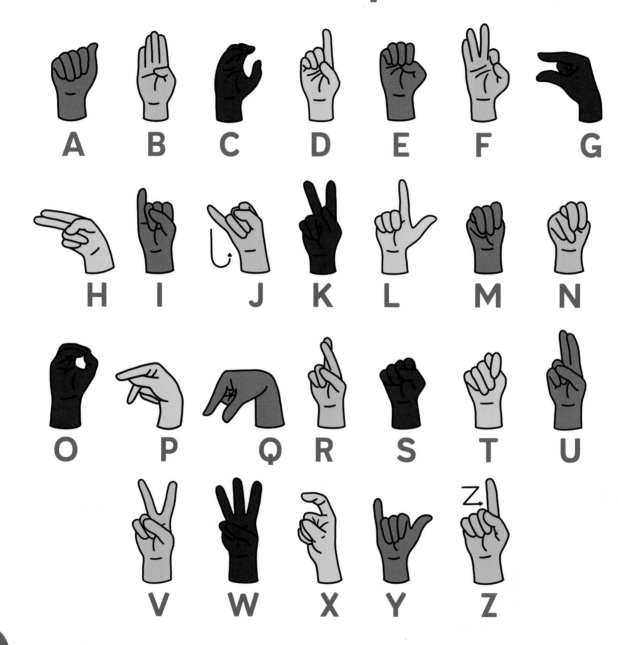

Glossary

ASL
short for American Sign Language, a language used by many deaf people in North America.

explore
to travel through in order to discover new things.

Index

Abdo Kids
ONLINE
FREE! ONLINE MULTIMEDIA RESOURCES

Visit **abdokids.com** to access crafts, games, videos, and more!

Use Abdo Kids code
ESK7014
or scan this QR code!